HUNTING AND FISHING

GOING BOWHUNTING

BY FELIX PETERS

Gareth Stevens Publishing

Please visit our website, www.garethstevens.com. For a free color catalog of all our high-quality books, call toll free 1-800-542-2595 or fax 1-877-542-2596.

Cataloging-in-Publication Data
Names: Peters, Felix.
Title: Going bowhunting / Felix Peters.
Description: Buffalo, NY : Gareth Stevens Publishing, 2027. | Series: Hunting and fishing | Includes glossary and index.
Identifiers: ISBN 9781482482492 (pbk.) | ISBN 9781482482508 (library bound) | ISBN 9781482482515 (ebook)
Subjects: LCSH: Bowhunting--Juvenile literature.
Classification: LCC SK36.P484 2027 | DDC 799.215--dc23

Published in 2027
Gareth Stevens Publishing
2544 Clinton Street
Buffalo, NY 14224

Portions of this work were originally authored by Tyler Omoth and published as *Bowhunting*. All new material in this edition was authored by Felix Peters.

Designer: Joshua Olson
Editor: Noah Riccardi

Photo credits: Cover, p. 1 Serhii Dubenets/Shutterstock.com; pp. 4–5 Viktor Cap/iStockphoto; p. 6 W. Scott McGill/Shutterstock.com; p. 8 Zoran Orcik/Shutterstock.com; p. 10 spxChrome/iStockphoto; p. 12 Hilde Anna/iStockphoto; p. 16 loonger/iStockphoto; p. 17 Maleo Photography/Shutterstock.com; p. 19 Bruce MacQueen/Shutterstock.com; p. 20 Windzepher/iStockphoto; p. 23 Jeffrey B. Banke/Shutterstock.com; p. 24 NaturesMomentsuk/Shutterstock.com; p. 26 Lakkana Savaksuriyawong/Shutterstock.com; p. 29 Ondrej Prosicky/Shutterstock.com.

Printed in China

Some of the images in this book illustrate individuals who are models. The depictions do not imply actual situations or events.

CPSIA compliance information: Batch #QS27GS: For further information contact Gareth Stevens at 1-800-542-2595.

TABLE OF CONTENTS

CHAPTER 1

BOWHUNTING THEN AND NOW

Bows were invented thousands of years ago. People shaped flexible pieces of wood into bows. They fitted the bows with strings. Bows allowed people to fire arrows at any target. Hunters no longer had to get close enough to an animal to throw a spear. Instead, they could fire arrows at animals from farther away.

Shooting arrows with a bow is called archery.

Early arrowheads were often made from stone such as flint.

As a result, hunters no longer had to put themselves in as much danger.

Hunting rifles were developed in the 1800s. This new way to hunt was much easier than bowhunting. But many people still enjoyed the challenge of hunting with bows and arrows.

Early arrows were made of wood. But in 1939, aluminum arrows were introduced. These metal arrows were stronger and lighter.

People also invented stronger bows. The first compound bow was created in 1966. It used a series of **pulleys**. This made it possible for hunters to shoot farther and with more force than ever before.

Hundreds of years after the hunting rifle was invented, bowhunting lives on. Every year, millions of people take to the woods to bowhunt.

CHAPTER 2

BOWHUNTING 101

Bowhunters enjoy hunting a wide variety of animals. Deer, elk, and moose are popular targets. Other hunters pursue mountain goats or turkeys. Some bowhunters even shoot bears.

Hunters carry their arrows in a container called a quiver. Arrow tips that people use for hunting are called broadheads.

Wearing camouflage clothing helps hunters blend in with their surroundings.

A broadhead arrow tip is extremely sharp.

Broadheads are larger than the arrow tips used by archers who shoot at targets. Their sharp points help hunters make clean kills.

A traditional bow uses a string attached to a frame. The frame is made from flexible materials such as wood. As the hunter **draws** the bowstring back, the bow's frame flexes. This adds tension to the string. When the hunter releases the string, the tension is released, too. This sends the arrow forward.

Some hunters use compound bows. A compound bow's pulleys make it easier for the hunter to pull back the string. Pulleys also increase the **thrust** of the arrow. As a result, hunters who use compound bows are able to shoot game from farther away. They can also take down bigger animals than hunters using traditional bows.

Some hunters carry their tree stands on their backs.

Tree stands help bowhunters get good shots. Hunters set up tree stands near areas where animals often come. Being up in a stand gives the hunter a clear line of sight. The view from a tree stand should always be free of branches that could block the shot.

Hunters may use lure scents to bring animals closer to their stands. They may also use cover scents to make sure animals will not smell them.

Binoculars help hunters see animals that are far away. A hunting knife is a useful tool that every hunter should carry as well.

GAME CALLS

One of the best ways to lure game closer is to use a call. Each type of animal has several different calls. Some calls are loud and aggressive. Others are soft. By learning the different calls and when to use them, hunters can bring in their game for a great shot.

CHAPTER 3

GETTING READY

Bowhunting requires patience and a lot of practice. Hunting with a bow can be more difficult than hunting with a gun for several reasons. Bows are not as powerful as guns. They are less accurate at long distances. Because of these limitations, it is important for bowhunters to aim carefully.

People often practice their shooting skills at archery ranges.

A bow's draw weight is important. The draw weight is the amount of pressure needed to pull back the bow's string. The harder it is to draw the string, the more power the shot will have.

Hunters should choose the correct draw weight based on the type of animal they are hunting. Some areas have laws that

ARCHERY RANGES

At archery ranges, hunters practice shooting a bow and aiming for targets. Some hunters use targets shaped like deer, bears, or other animals. These lifelike targets help hunters practice shots that will make a clean kill. Hunters learn the best places to aim for each kind of animal.

Targets shaped like animals help hunters practice their aim before hunts.

declare a minimum draw weight. Each hunter should make sure that his or her bow is up to the task. A bow that is too weak may injure an animal without making a clean kill.

A shot to the heart or lungs of an animal is the surest way to get a clean kill. For most four-legged animals, such as deer or bears, a hunter should aim just behind the animal's shoulder. But each animal has a slightly different **anatomy**. Hunters should study the best kill shots for each kind of animal they hunt.

Hunters should also look for potential hunting areas before the season begins. When **scouting**, hunters look for an area where there are many animals. It can be hard to see the animals themselves, so hunters often look for signs of animal activity. Footprints, clearly worn paths, and **scat** show that animals are nearby.

Matted grass and flattened leaves are common signs of deer beds, or places where deer have lain down.

Large, flattened patches of grass may show that animals have rested in the area.

Some signs indicate the presence of particular animals. For example, deer and elk scrape their antlers on trees. This creates obvious marks. Bears also claw at trees to mark their territory.

CHAPTER 4

STAYING SAFE

When a bow's string is released, it can snap along the hunter's arm. To prevent injuries, a hunter should wear an arm guard. This protective sleeve goes on the hunter's extended arm. The string can also sting the hunter's fingers. Because of this, many hunters wear archery gloves.

Many archery gloves have only three fingers.

Leather guards on the gloves' fingers protect hunters' hands.

The arrows used for hunting are extremely sharp. They should never be carried loose or **nocked** in a bow. Instead, hunters should store their arrows in a quiver. They should keep the quiver's top closed until they are ready to shoot.

Climbing into a tree stand while carrying a bow and quiver is dangerous. Instead, hunters should use a rope to pull up the bow and quiver after them.

Each hunter in a tree stand should wear a safety harness, too. The harness secures the hunter to the tree and helps prevent falls.

A hunter pulls up his bow with a rope.

CHAPTER 5

LAWS OF HUNTING

Each area has its own hunting seasons and regulations. Governments make these laws to protect animals. Hunting seasons vary for different **species** of animals. Bowhunters should learn and follow the laws for the kinds of animals they plan to hunt. Bowhunters must also buy the appropriate hunting licenses.

Some programs that protect wildlife get their funding from hunting license sales.

Hunters look for paw prints to track wounded animals.

Money from license sales is used to **preserve** the animals' **habitats**.

Hunters should respect natural areas during the hunt. They should not leave anything behind at their hunting site. This includes arrows. Fired arrows can be hard to find. But hunters should never leave them out in the woods. Hunters should also track down any animals they shoot.

Bowhunting is an activity that has survived for thousands of years. By following hunting guidelines, bowhunters help make sure that this thrilling activity will be around for many more.

TRACKING AN ANIMAL

Hunters must be careful when tracking a wounded animal. They should always be prepared to find cover in case there are other animals nearby that could attack. Hunters should be careful when they find the animal, too. An animal with its eyes closed is likely still alive. It could still injure the hunter.

FACT FILE

OUT IN THE MOUNTAINS

In the United States, the Mountain West region is known as a good bowhunting area. States such as Colorado, Wyoming, Montana, and Idaho have lots of public land and few people. Those areas of open land are great for bowhunting.

In the Mountain West, hunters can find bears, deer, wolves, and even mountain lions. Hunting mountain lions can be especially hard. That's because they can be tough to find. They can also escape easily.

Hunters often use dogs to track mountain lions. Dogs can track mountain lions by scent. Once they catch an animal's scent, they chase it. The dogs run after the mountain lion until it goes into a tree.

Snow can make hunting mountain lions easier. It can help hunters see the animals' tracks.

Then the hunter can approach. They find a good spot and try to shoot the mountain lion.

TEST YOUR KNOWLEDGE

Take this quiz to test your knowledge.

1. Write a letter to a friend describing the main ideas of Chapter 4.

2. Why do you think people continued to hunt with bows after rifles were invented?

3. How is a compound bow different from a regular bow?

    A. A compound bow uses a set of pulleys.
    B. A compound bow fires arrows from four strings at once.
    C. A compound bow has more than one frame.

4. Why would a tree stand help a bowhunter get a good shot?

    A. It blocks noises that could distract the hunter.
    B. It helps the hunter focus on a smaller area.
    C. It lifts the hunter above bushes and branches.

Answers can be found on page 32.

GLOSSARY

anatomy
The physical structure of a living thing.

draws
Pulls back the string on a bow.

habitats
The type of places where plants or animals normally grow or live.

nocked
When an arrow is fitted to the bowstring in preparation for shooting.

preserve
To protect something so that it does not change.

pulleys
Wheels with grooves that ropes or chains run through.

scat
The waste of an animal.

scouting
Looking for signs of animals.

species
A group of animals or plants that are similar.

thrust
The forward force of a launched object.

FOR MORE INFORMATION

BOOKS

Brach, Kyle. *Bowhunting*. Minneapolis, MN: Lerner Publications, 2024.

Conley, Kate. *The Hunting Encyclopedia*. Minneapolis, MN: Abdo Publishing, 2024.

WEBSITES

Britannica Kids: American Black Bear
kids.britannica.com/kids/article/American-black-bear/638854
Learn more about a common bowhunting target.

National Geographic Kids: Wyoming
kids.nationalgeographic.com/geography/states/article/wyoming
Learn more about a popular bowhunting destination.

Publisher's note to educators and parents: Our editors have carefully reviewed these websites to ensure that they are suitable for students. Many websites change frequently, however, and we cannot guarantee that a site's future contents will continue to meet our high standards of quality and educational value. Be advised that students should be closely supervised whenever they access the internet.

INDEX

Answer Key: 1. Answers will vary; 2. Answers will vary; 3. A; 4. C